PASSPORT TO

RUSSIA

Keith Lye

Franklin Watts

A Division of Grolier Publishing

New York • London • Hong Kong • Sydney

Danbury, Connecticut

Copyright © 1996 Watts Books
Original Edition 1987

This American Edition © 1996 by
Franklin Watts
A Division of Grolier Publishing
Sherman Turnpike
Danbury, Connecticut 06816

Library of Congress Cataloging-in-
Publication Data

Lye, Keith.
   Passport to Russia / by Keith Lye.
    p. cm. — (Passport to)
   Includes index.
   ISBN 0-531-14384-8
   1. Russia (Federation)—Juvenile literature   I. Title.
II. Series.
DK510.23.L96 1995
947—dc20   95-11603
                                        CIP AC

Editor: Belinda Weber
Design: Val Carless
Illustrations: Gary Cookson
               Hayward Art Group

Photographs: Novosti 6B, 6T, 7T 8T, 9TL,
9TR, 9CL, 9CR, 9LR, 11B, 12T, 1±3T, 16B,
17TL, 17TR, 18T, 19T, 20T, 22T, 24T, 24B,
25TL, 25B, 28, 29TL, 29TR, 29C, 29B, 30T,
30B, 31T, 31B, 32T, 32B, 33T, 33C, 33B, 34T,
34BL, 34BR, 38T, 38BR, 39B, 40B, 41B, 43B,
44T, 44B, 45TL; Chris Fairclough: 20B, 25TR;
Hutchison Picture Library: 5T, 9B, 13B, Q9B,
35T; Stephen Keeler: 17B, 21B, 45TR; Kobal
Collection: 41TR; Popperfoto: 42BL, 42R, 45B;
John Massey Stewart: 7B, 22B, 23B, 42T,
43TL, 43TR; Zefa: 5B, 8B, 10T, 10B, 11TL,
11TR, 16T, 18B, 21T, 23T, 35B, 38BL, 39T, 40T,
41TL.

Contents

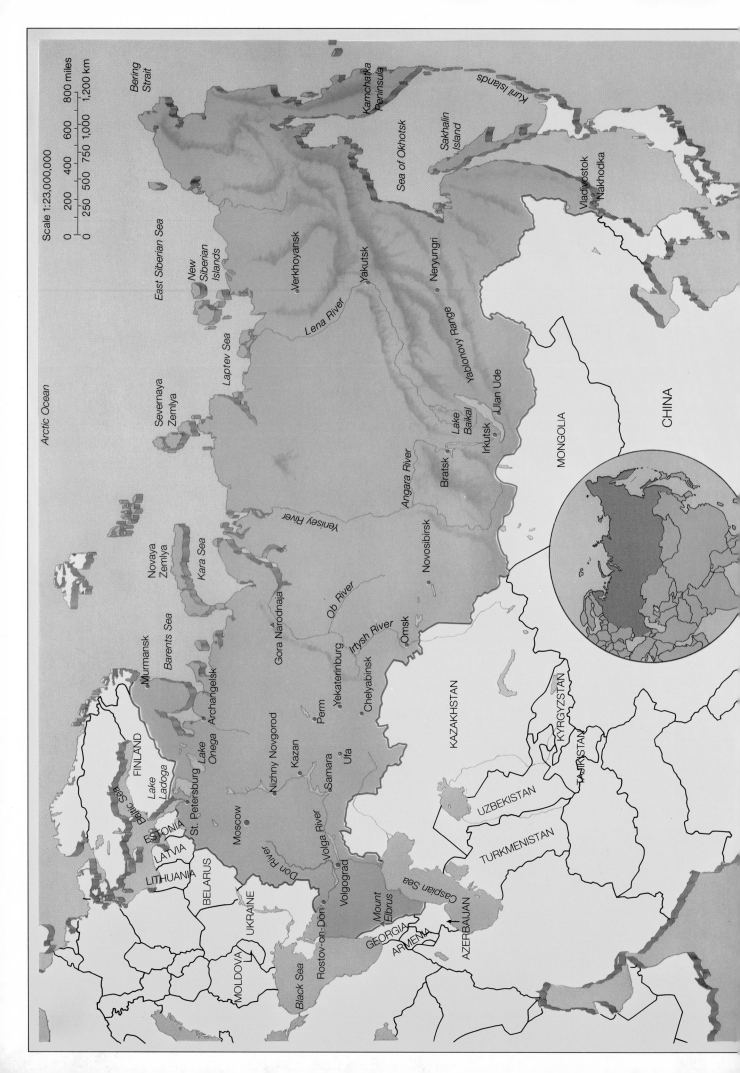

Scale 1:23,000,000

	miles
0 200 400 600 800	
0 250 500 750 1,000 1,200 km	

Bering Strait

Arctic Ocean

East Siberian Sea

New Siberian Islands

Kamchatka Peninsula

Kuril Islands

Sea of Okhotsk

Sakhalin Island

Verkhoyansk

Lena River

Yakutsk

Neryungri

Laptev Sea

Severnaya Zemlya

Yablonovy Range

Vladivostok
Nakhodka

Ulan Ude

Lake Baikal

Irkutsk

Angara River

Bratsk

Novaya Zemlya

Kara Sea

Yenisey River

Novosibirsk

MONGOLIA

CHINA

Murmansk

Barents Sea

Archangelsk

Gora Narodnaja

Ob River

Irtysh River

Omsk

Yekaterinburg

Chelyabinsk

KAZAKHSTAN

Perm

Finland

Lake Onega

Lake Ladoga

Nizhny Novgorod

Kazan

Samara

Ufa

Baltic Sea

ESTONIA

St. Petersburg

LATVIA

Moscow

LITHUANIA

BELARUS

Volga River

Don River

UKRAINE

MOLDOVA

Volgograd

Rostov-on-Don

Mount Elbrus

Black Sea

GEORGIA

ARMENIA

Caspian Sea

AZERBAIJAN

TURKMENISTAN

UZBEKISTAN

TAJIKISTAN

KYRGYZSTAN

Introduction

Russia, which is also officially called the Russian Federation, is the world's largest country. It covers about an eighth of the world's land area and is nearly twice the size of Canada, the second largest country. Russia extends across two continents. About 25 percent of its land area is in Europe, and the rest is in Asia.

From 1922, Russia was part of the Union of Soviet Socialist Republics (USSR). The USSR, or Soviet Union, was a Communist country, made up of 15 republics. In 1991, following the failure of Soviet economic policies, the country's 15 republics split to become separate countries, the largest of which is Russia.

Twelve of these republics, excluding the Baltic states of Estonia, Latvia, and Lithuania, keep in contact through an organization called the Commonwealth of Independent States (CIS). Since 1991, Russia has faced many problems in reforming its economy and building a free enterprise system.

Above: These houses on the shores of Lake Baikal are built to withstand the cold. They are typical of those in the more remote Russian regions.

Below: Old churches, factories, modern offices, and apartments can all be seen in this view of Moscow, Russia's capital and largest city.

The land

Russia stretches from the Baltic Sea in the west to the Pacific Ocean in the east. The maximum east-west distance is about 6,000 miles (9,700 km). Russia includes eleven time zones. At breakfast time in Vladivostok, in the far east, it is late afternoon in Moscow. From north to south, Russia extends from the icy Arctic Ocean to the warm shores of the Black and Caspian seas. The greatest north-south distance is over 2,500 miles (4,000 km).

Most of Russia has long, cold, snowy winters and warm or hot summers. At Verkhoyansk, in the northeast, temperatures vary between –90°F (–68°C) in winter and 98°F (37°C) in summer. The warmest regions are in the southwest, between the Caspian and Black seas.

The precipitation (rain, snow, sleet, and other forms of moisture) is generally light. Parts of the southwest and northeast have dry climates, with an average of less than 8 inches (20 cm) per year. The European plains in the west and the mountain regions throughout Russia have the greatest precipitation.

Above: No trees grow on the tundra, only small shrubs, grasses and lichens. Even in summer the ground just below the topsoil is frozen solid.

Below: A view of the bleak countryside of Sakhalin Island in eastern Siberia. The mountains are surrounded by taiga, forests of coniferous trees.

The far north is mostly a frozen, treeless plain bordering the Arctic Ocean. This is the tundra. In summer, the top few inches of soil thaw, but below that lies the permafrost, ground that never thaws. South of the tundra lies the world's largest forest, called the taiga. Conifers, such as Siberian larches, are the main trees in the taiga. South of the forests are grasslands, called steppes. Semidesert and mountains lie in the far south.

Most of European Russia is flat or gently rolling country. In the south lie the Caucasus Mountains, containing Russia's highest point, Mount Elbrus. Asian Russia, east of the low Ural Mountains, is called Siberia. It is a vast region of plains, plateaus, and mountains, with active volcanoes in the Kamchatka peninsula. Russia contains the world's deepest lake, Baikal, and part of the world's largest inland body of water, the Caspian Sea. Major rivers include the Lena and the Volga.

Above: A view of the Yenisey River as it flows through Krasnoyarsk in Siberia.

Below: Russian cowboys moving cattle through the grasslands of steppe country.

The people

About 82 percent of the people in Russia are of Russian ancestry. They are the descendants of a group of people called the Slavs who lived in eastern Europe thousands of years ago. Historians divide the Slavs into three main groups: the East Slavs, the West Slavs, and the South Slavs. The Russians are descended from the East Slavs. These people founded the first Russian state, called Kievan Rus, in the ninth century. After the Mongols defeated Kievan Rus in the thirteenth century, Moscow became the center of Russian power.

Russian is the official language. It is written in the Cyrillic alphabet. This alphabet has letters that are written and pronounced differently from those of the Roman alphabet.

Russia has about one hundred ethnic groups. Minority groups include Tatars, Ukrainians, Chuvashes, Bashkirs, Belorussians, Mordovians, Chechens, Germans, Udmurts, Mari, Kazakhs, Avars, Armenians, and Jews. Small groups of Aleuts, Chukchi, Inuit (Eskimo), and Koryaks live in the far north of Siberia.

Above: An old woman and a child from Sakhalin Island. Their features show that they are descendants of original Mongol inhabitants.

Below: A general view of the river flowing through St. Petersburg. In the foreground one of its large parks can be seen.

Above: Schoolchildren aged between 7-8 learn about computers.

Below: A construction worker from Buryat Autonomous Republic.

Above: Andrei Bogachev is a traffic policeman in Moscow.

Below: Weaver Valentina Golubeva training workers at Ivanovo.

Many of Russia's minority groups have their own language, speaking Russian as their second language. Because of its mixed population, Russia is a federation consisting of 21 republics, 6 territories, 49 provinces, 10 autonomous (self-governing) areas, 2 cities with federal status (Moscow and St. Petersburg), and the autonomous Jewish region of Birobijan in the far southeast. In the early 1990s, some minority peoples asked for a greater degree of self-rule. For example, the Chechens declared their area, the Chechen Republic, independent in 1991. But Russia did not recognize this act.

Religious worship was discouraged when Russia was under Communist rule. But from the late 1980s, the government allowed religious groups to organize. Church attendance increased quickly. The chief religious group is the Russian Orthodox Church. Other groups include Roman Catholics, Protestants, Muslims, and Jews.

Above: An outdoor bookstall in Nizhny-Novgorod.

Below: Children in traditional uniform at an elementary school.

Where people live

In 1993, Russia had a population of about 148 million. Only China, India, the United States, Indonesia, and Brazil have larger populations. Almost 80 percent of the people live in European Russia, which has a population density of about 72 per square mile (28 per sq km). By contrast, Siberia has an average population density of only 5 people per square mile (2 per sq km).

Increased mechanization and efficiency in agriculture has meant that fewer farmworkers are needed than in the past and so many young people have moved into urban areas, where living conditions and leisure facilities are usually better. As a result, Russia has become an urbanized country, with 74 percent of the people in the cities and towns. Moscow and St. Petersburg are the largest cities. Russia also has eleven other cities with populations of more than 1,000,000 and more than thirty with populations of over 500,000.

Above: A typical wooden peasant cottage with a green picket fence in Moscow.

Below: Moscow apartments. Migration to the cities has caused overcrowding.

Left: The old section of town, Ulyanovsk.

Above: Houses at Listvyanka, a village near Irkutsk on the shores of Lake Baikal.

Below: A motorized sled roars over the snow in the Kamchatka Peninsula of eastern Siberia. Such vehicles have made life easier in the harsh climate.

Migration from the countryside to the cities, especially Moscow, the most popular destination, has produced labor shortages in some remote areas. During the Communist period, the government offered special facilities to attract people to eastern Siberia and live in new settlements to develop the area's rich natural resources. Meanwhile, the cities became overcrowded. The situation became worse during World War II (1939–1945), when over a million houses and apartment buildings were destroyed.

Housing shortages continue to this day. For example, about a fifth of city dwellers have to share their homes with another family. Most urban people live in rented apartments or small houses. Few own their homes, and young married couples have to wait for several years before getting their own apartment. However, private ownership has been encouraged since the breakup of the former Soviet Union in 1991.

In rural areas, many families have their own houses, though some remote areas lack such facilities as electricity, gas, and running water.

Moscow

Moscow became the national capital of what was to become the Soviet Union in 1918. But the origins of the city go back about 800 years, when settlers on the north bank of the Moskva River, where Moscow stands today, built a *kreml* — a walled fortress. Inside were important buildings, such as churches, a palace, and arsenals. Several Russian cities began as kremlins (the English form of *kreml*).

The Moscow Kremlin is the seat of Russia's national government. In it are magnificent domed churches and cathedrals, a former royal palace, museums, and government offices. The Kremlin Palace of Congresses, completed in 1961, was the meeting place of the Soviet Communist party from 1961 to 1990.

Moscow is a city of theaters, concert halls, movie houses, museums, and libraries. Muscovites think of themselves as the most cultured people in Russia, though the people of Russia's former capital of St. Petersburg (called Leningrad in Communist times) challenge this claim.

Above: St. Basil's Cathedral, Red Square, in the heart of Moscow, is made up of nine chapels each with its own elaborately decorated roof.

Below: Some of the landmarks of Moscow. They show the contrast between the old part of the city and the new capital.

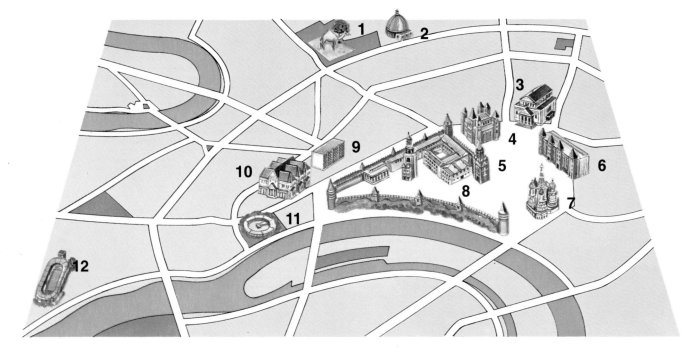

1. Zoo	**4.** Museum	**7.** St. Basil's Cathedral	**10.** Fine Arts Museum
2. Planetarium	**5.** Red Square	**8.** The Kremlin	**11.** Swimming Pool
3. Bolshoi Theatre	**6.** Gum	**9.** Library	**12.** Sports Stadium

Northeast of the Kremlin is Red Square, where the former Communist government held huge parades on special occasions. Landmarks in Red Square include St. Basil's Cathedral and, beneath the Kremlin's eastern wall, a mausoleum where visitors can view the embalmed body of Vladimir Lenin, leader of the Communist Russian Revolution in 1917.

The Moscow Metro is the most elegant subway line in the world. Its 141 stations, decorated with marble, granite, and crystal, are kept spotless by armies of cleaning people. It carries about 7,000,000 passengers a day along its 141 miles (227 km) of track.

Muscovites eat about 170 tons of ice cream every day, even when winter temperatures drop to 14°F (–10°C). They are also animal lovers who keep thousands of cats, dogs, and birds. Like other Soviet city dwellers, they like to spend much of their leisure time in the surrounding countryside. Some are lucky enough to own a dacha, a country cottage.

Above: Arbat, in the older part of Moscow, was the first street in the city for pedestrians only. In nice weather it is full of people shopping.

Below: Even in late spring snow, Moscow citizens like to drink their coffee or chocolate at an open-air cafe.

Fact file: land and population

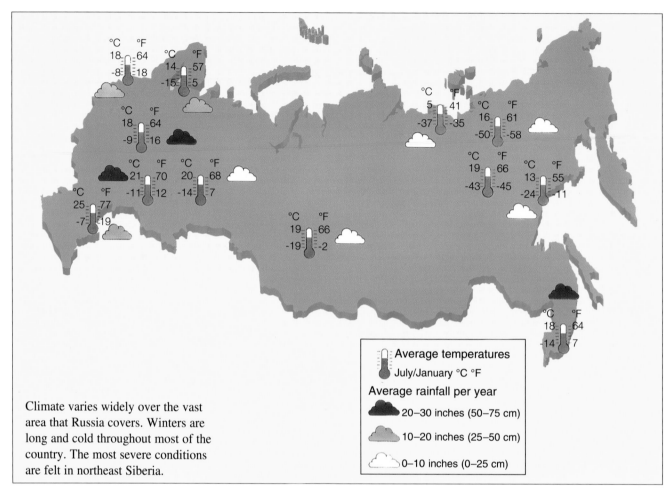

Climate varies widely over the vast area that Russia covers. Winters are long and cold throughout most of the country. The most severe conditions are felt in northeast Siberia.

Average temperatures
July/January °C °F
Average rainfall per year
20–30 inches (50–75 cm)
10–20 inches (25–50 cm)
0–10 inches (0–25 cm)

▷ **Land area comparison**
With an area of 6,592,850 square miles (17,075,400 sq km) Russia is nearly twice as big as the United States and seventy times larger than the United Kingdom.

RUSSIA   **U.S.**   **AUSTRALIA**   **U.K.**

Key Facts

Location: Russia is the world's largest country. It straddles Europe and Asia. The mainland extends roughly between latitudes 41° south and over 80° north and between longitudes 28° east and 170° west.
Area: 6,592,850 square miles (17,075,400 sq km)
Population: 148,000,000 (1993)
Capital: Moscow

Major cities
(with populations):
Moscow (8,747,000)
St. Petersburg
  (formerly Leningrad, 4,437,000)
Novosibirsk (1,442,000)
Nizhny Novgorod
  (formerly Gorki, 1,441,000)
Yekaterinburg
(formerly Sverdlovsk, 1,371,000)

Highest point: Mount Elbrus in the Caucasus Mountains 18,520 feet (5,642 m) above sea level.
Longest river: (entirely within Russia): Lena, 2,734 miles (4,400 km); (longest in the European part of Russia): Volga, 2,194 miles (3,531 km).
Largest body of inland water: Caspian Sea, which has a total area of 143,000 square miles (370,370 sq km).

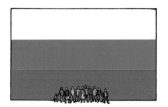

Russia 23 per square mile

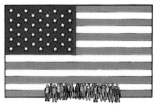

U.S. 70 per square mile

Australia 5 per square mile

Britain 608 per square mile

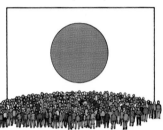

Japan 866 per square mile

France 273 per square mile

▽ **Where people live**
Nearly three times as many people live
in cities and towns as in rural areas.

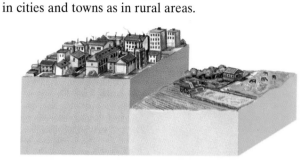

◁ **A population density comparison**
In world terms, Russia's population
density is extremely low. This is because
so much of Asian Russia (Siberia) is
almost empty of people.

St. Petersburg

Moscow

Nizhny Novgorod

Samara

Yekaterinburg

Novosibirsk

 Major cities
--- Main routeways

△ **Major population centers**
Most of Russia's largest cities are
situated in the western (European) part
of the country, where the main industrial
areas are found.

Home life

In 1991, the birth rate in Russia was estimated to be 12 per 1,000 people, which is less than half of the world average figure. One reason for the low birth rate is the shortage of good housing in the inner cities.

The housing shortage was also one of the causes of the social discontent that led to the introduction of reforms in the Soviet Union in the 1980s. For example, in 1987, an estimated 17 percent of Soviet citizens did not have their own dwelling. Many newly married couples have to live with their parents for several years before they can find a home of their own. In 1937, experts estimated that a couple wanting state housing had to wait ten to fifteen years before they were accommodated.

The average family apartment in Russia has two rooms, used for both living and sleeping. The apartment also contains a small, eat-in kitchen, a bathroom, a toilet, a small entrance hall, and perhaps a balcony.

Above: A Russian family dining in a typical town apartment in Satka, south of the Ural Mountains.

Right: Weddings are a time for celebration. This happy wedding party with three married couples is crossing Red Square in the heart of Moscow.

Under Communist rule, the production of consumer goods had a lower priority than heavy industry. As a result, many household items, common in Western homes, were often difficult to obtain in the Soviet Union. Since the reforms of the 1980s and the breakup of the Soviet Union in 1991, standards of living have improved, especially for people in the bottom 10 percent of the population. But some popular domestic items, such as video recorders, remain in short supply.

More than 90 percent of Russian families now have a refrigerator and 80 percent have a washing machine. Almost all families have a television set, though many are still black-and-white. Nearly one-fifth of households own a car and nearly 70 percent have a bicycle.

Health care remains free, though private health-care services are developing. Officially unemployment is low, but this is partly the result of government aid to industries that may eventually disappear as competition increases in the new Russia, with its increasingly free enterprise economy.

Above left: Birthdays are a time for celebration. Here a grandmother poses for a photograph surrounded by her children and grandchildren.

Above: A five-year-old's birthday party in her family's Moscow apartment.

Below: Cats are popular family pets among people who live in cities.

Stores and shopping

Shopping in Russian cities and towns can be an exhausting business. Until recently all stores used the "three-line" system. Under it, customers line up to order the goods they want to buy. The shop assistant removes the goods from the shelf or display case, writes the order on a ticket and hands it to the customer. The customer then waits at the cash desk to pay for the goods. The cashier takes the money and stamps the ticket. The customer returns to sales counter for another long wait to give the stamped ticket to the assistant, who hands over the goods, usually wrapped in paper and tied with string.

This tedious and time-consuming system is still used in many toy stores, bookstores, and some clothing and food stores. It has been replaced in the large department stores and new food supermarkets in some of the larger cities by the Western system of paying at the counter or checkout. From the 1980s, stores have been better stocked, but long lines of people waiting to buy what they need are still common sights throughout Russia.

Above: Farmers selling their produce by the side of the road. This is popular in small villages and rural areas.

Left: A McDonald's restaurant in Moscow. Familiar Western fast-food restaurants are becoming more popular in Russia's larger cities.

Left: Inside Cheryomushki supermarket in Moscow. In such supermarkets the Western system of paying at checkout desks has been introduced, which cuts down on shopping time.

Below: GUM is Moscow's largest department store. It stands on Red Square, opposite the Kremlin. GUM stands for Gosudartsvenniy Universalniy Magazin (State Department Store).

Russia still has difficulty in distributing food and consumer products so that they reach everyone. Efficient distribution and rising prices are two major problems faced by Russian shoppers in the 1990s.

Grandparents often help out with the shopping. While the rest of the family is at school or at work these older members can search the stores and markets for newly delivered foodstuffs.

Although such searching is becoming less necessary as food distribution improves, few women – who do most of the shopping – go out without carrying a bag so they can take advantage of unexpected supplies in the stores.

One of the less desirable developments arising from Russia's gradual change from a Communist to a free enterprise economy has been the growth of a "black economy." This enables citizens to buy almost anything they want, if they can afford the black market prices.

Cooking and eating

The food eaten by Russian citizens is traditional. It reflects their various ethnic origins — although pizza and hamburger bars are now appearing in Moscow.

Breakfast is a quick, light meal. It may consist of slices of rye bread, a piece of cheese, and tea. Dinner, the main meal of the day, includes a meat dish with potatoes and other vegetables. This may be followed by a simple dessert of fresh fruit or cake. Russians are fond of meat, so supper will probably include another meat dish, after a bowl of shchi (cabbage soup). People eat large quantities of bread and drink sweet black tea with most meals.

No Russian table is complete without its samovar, an urn in which water is boiled to make tea. The teapot itself usually sits on top of the samovar to keep hot.

Above: A selection of the kind of foods that Russian people like to eat. They include fresh salads, roast pork, and a mug of rich soup.

Right: A typical family meal in Russia. The ornate samovar (tea urn) dominating the table is a very common sight in Russian homes. People throughout Russia drink sweet black tea.

Left: A traditional Kasha festival near Zainsk. Kasha is a dish made from crushed or powdered buckwheat. It is usually baked in the oven, then mixed with butter.

Below: A poster warning against alcoholism. Russian citizens used to drink more hard liquor than people in many other countries.

Traditional Russian dishes include borscht, a pungent soup made with chopped beets, onions, tomatoes, shredded cabbage, and diced sausages. Meat stock, herbs, and slivers of mutton or beef are added, and the borscht is served with sour cream. It may be followed by hot piroshki (meat-filled pastries) and sweet blini (pancakes with jam and sour cream).

Traditionally meals were washed down with iced vodka. Until recently Soviet citizens drank more alcoholic spirits than any other people — an average of 30 pints (14 liters) a year for every person aged over fifteen. In 1985 the price of vodka was quadrupled as part of the government's intensive anti-drinking campaign. The campaign has been successful in the towns, but less so in the countryside where illegal vodka is distilled.

In the early 1990s, rising prices caused by inflation and economic reforms led to changes in Russian eating habits. Bread and egg consumption increased at the expense of meat and fruits. Also, people tend to be less hospitable than in the past, when inviting friends and relatives to meals was an important part of social life.

Pastimes and sports

Chess is the most popular pastime in Russia, and millions of people learn to play the game to a high standard at an early age. In summer open-air chess games in parks or on quiet street corners are a common sight. They attract large crowds of spectators, young and old, who follow each move with fascination. The country has produced many grandmasters and about a dozen world champions, among them Gary Kasparov and Anatoly Karpov.

Another popular pastime is stamp collecting and there are thousands of stamp clubs.

Millions of Russians enjoy going to the movies. In the 1980s, the Soviet Union produced about 180 feature films a year. In 1991, the number soared to 400. But then, production shrank as a result of the proposed breakup of government-supported film organizations. Russia also has many museums, which are popular attractions with families. Some, like the Hermitage Museum in St. Petersburg, attract visitors from all over the world.

Above: In warm weather people flock to lakeside and seaside resorts around the Black Sea to swim. Some people even bathe in the ice-covered rivers.

Below: Soccer is popular throughout Russia, from local teams that play in parks to the country's successful international teams.

Left: Lakes in Siberia freeze solid in winter and are safe for children to play on. Here a group of children are skating, sleighing, and trying to play ice hockey.

Below: Spectators take a keen interest as people play chess at Gorky Park, Moscow.

More than half the people take an annual vacation. Moscow and the sunny Black Sea resorts are the favorite places. Travel is relatively cheap. Travel companies belong to the state or such organizations as trade unions.

Organized sports play an important part in the daily life of most Russian citizens. There are thousands of physical training clubs, sports halls, swimming pools, and stadiums, all of which are open free to all citizens. Schools also encourage physical education. It is hardly surprising that Russians win so many medals for sports and gymnastics in international competitions. Soccer is the leading sport. Track and field events, volleyball, and basketball are all popular, while ice hockey, skating, and skiing attract many people in winter.

Ethnic minorities also have their own traditional forms of exercise. The Yakuts of central Siberia are skilled reindeer-sled racers; archery is popular with the Buryats of eastern Siberia; and on the Amur River in southeastern Russia, canoeing is a popular sport.

News and broadcasting

Before 1917 more than 75 percent of the Russian people were illiterate. Today almost everyone can read. People spend, on average, almost one-sixth of their free time doing so. To meet this demand, Russia has become a major producer of newspapers, magazines, and books. Under Communist rule, the media, which could be very influential, was heavily censored by the government.

In 1991, the press law encouraged the growth of the publishing industry. The readership of radical publications soared, while the number of subscribers to official Communist newspapers fell dramatically. By 1992, Russia had more than 4,800 officially registered newspapers and more than 3,500 periodicals. Leading dailies include *Izvestiya, Komosomolskaya Pravda,* and *Trud.* In 1993, President Boris Yeltsin announced the banning of several newspapers and the dismissals of the editors of *Pravda*, the old Communist Party paper, and *Sovetskaya Rossiya*, which expressed extreme nationalist views.

Above: Vladimir Nazarov, a Russian radio reporter, interviews workers on the twenty-fourth floor of a new apartment building that is under construction.

Below: Hosts Aza Likhitchenko and Igor Kirilov in a Moscow television studio. Russian television emphasizes serious and educational programs.

Above left: A selection of children's books, ranging from fairy tales to how-to books.

Above: Russian readers have plenty of magazines to choose from, covering all topics from serious political reading to tabloids.

Below: Some of the newspapers published when Russia was part of the Soviet Union. The Soviet media expressed the government's views.

Soviet radio and television services were more serious than those in the West. They broadcast many news and documentary programs, classic music, sports, and cartoons for children. Violence was censored, and most programs were educational.

Since 1990, censorship has been relaxed and advertising is now permitted. Television and radio broadcasting comes under the Russian Federal Television and Radio Broadcasting Service, established in 1993. The two main channels are Ostankino and All-Russian State Television. There are also local city channels. About 98 percent of Russians can receive TV broadcasts. Satellite TV reached 5 percent of the people in 1993. Cable TV is also available in some areas. Access to Western influences increased in the 1990s. Russian teenagers enjoy popular music, especially from Britain and the United States. Russia even has some rock bands, and in the last few years discos are becoming more common.

Fact file: home and leisure

Key Facts

Population composition: In 1992, people under 15 years of age made up 22.6 percent of the population; people between 15 and 59 made up 60.9 percent; and people over 60 made up 16.5 percent. Women formed 53 percent of the population.

Average life expectancy: 69 years in 1992. By comparison, people in the United States have an average life expectancy of 77 years, whereas people in India live, on average, 61 years. In 1992, Russian women had an average life expectancy of 75 years, 11 years longer than Russian men.

Rate of population increase: 0.5 percent per year between 1985 and 1992, as compared with the world average of 1.7 percent. On current trends, the population is expected to decline to about 145.2 million in the year 2010.

Family life: The marriage rate in 1991 was 8.6 per 1,000 people. The average number in a household was 3.2.

Homes: The average size of a town house or apartment is 152 square feet (14.1 sq m). Rents, payable to the state, are low at about 12 percent of net income.

Work: The total workforce in 1991 was 73,800,000, or 89.6 percent of people between 16 and 59. Women made up 52 percent of this figure. The five-day week was introduced in 1967, and the average working week is now 40 hours. The minimum wage in 1993 was 7,740 rubles per month.

Religions: Beginning in the late 1980s, many churches and monasteries were reopened and religious freedom restored under a "freedom of conscience" law. All religions are now equal before the law, and the main church, the Russian Orthodox Church, has an estimated 35 to 40 million adherents. Other groups include Protestants, Roman Catholics, Muslims, and Jews.

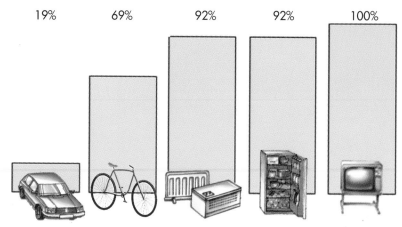

19%	69%	92%	92%	100%
Cars	Bicycles	Central heating	Refrigerator	Television

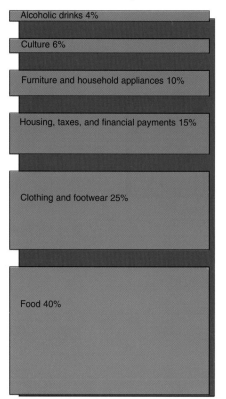

Alcoholic drinks 4%

Culture 6%

Furniture and household appliances 10%

Housing, taxes, and financial payments 15%

Clothing and footwear 25%

Food 40%

△ **How many households owned goods in 1992**
Ownership of household and other consumer goods has increased rapidly in recent years. Most homes have television sets, refrigerators, and central heating. But car ownership remains low by comparison with Western countries.

◁ **How the average household budget was spent in 1992**
Food accounts for a third of household spending in Russia. Expenditure on alcoholic drinks has declined in recent years because of a government campaign against alcohol abuse.

▽ **Soviet currency**
The unit of currency is the ruble, divided into 100 kopecks. In 1994, officially, U.S.$1 = 0.59 rubles (U.K. £1 = 0.87 rubles), but the market rate was $1 = 1,691 rubles (£1 = 2,520 rubles).

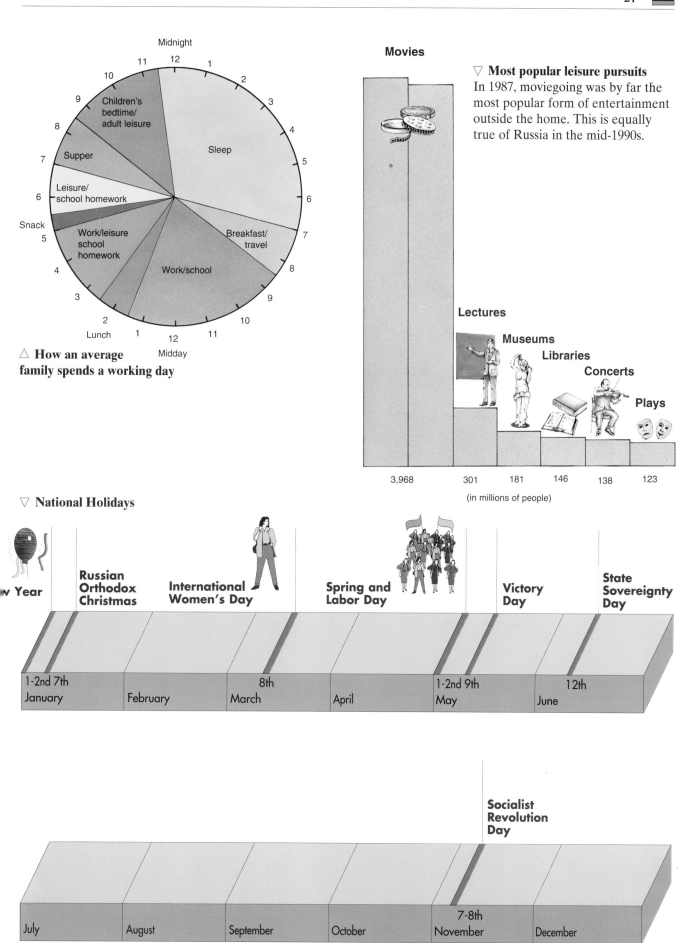

△ **How an average family spends a working day**

Midnight

Children's bedtime/adult leisure

Sleep

Supper

Leisure/school homework

Snack

Work/leisure school homework

Breakfast/travel

Work/school

Lunch

Midday

Movies

▽ **Most popular leisure pursuits**
In 1987, moviegoing was by far the most popular form of entertainment outside the home. This is equally true of Russia in the mid-1990s.

Lectures

Museums

Libraries

Concerts

Plays

3,968   301   181   146   138   123

(in millions of people)

▽ **National Holidays**

New Year

Russian Orthodox Christmas

International Women's Day

Spring and Labor Day

Victory Day

State Sovereignty Day

1-2nd 7th
January

February

8th
March

April

1-2nd 9th
May

12th
June

Socialist Revolution Day

July

August

September

October

7-8th
November

December

Farming and fishing

Under Communism, the government owned all farmland and industries. Farmland was divided between state farms and collectives. State farms employed workers who were paid by the state. Collective farms were jointly owned by all who worked on them, and wages were paid as equal shares out of the farm's profits. Each worker had a private plot for private use, which were often more productive than the land belonging to the collective.

When the Soviet Union broke up on 1991, private ownership of the land was permitted, and state farms and collectives were encouraged to register as cooperatives or share companies. By 1992, 77 percent of the former farms had reregistered, though some preferred to remain as state or collective farms.

In 1993, a law permitted free sale of land and the borrowing of money to develop it. But progress was slow in privatizing land ownership, and in some areas farmworkers banded together to set up private farms.

Above: A worker with a fine crop of peppers that have been grown in greenhouses on a collective farm in the Stavropol region, north of the Caucasus Mountains.

Right: Combine harvesters and other farm machinery are used on Russia's large wheat farms.

Russia has vast areas of fertile land, especially in the black earth region in the southern steppes. However, most of Russia has a short growing season. Droughts periodically affect 60 percent of Russia's best farmland, while occasional storms do much damage. When crops fail, Russia has to import food, especially grains. Yet in normal years, Russia is one of the world's leading producers of barley, oats, rye, and wheat.

Other major crops include flax, fruits, potatoes and other vegetables, sugar beet, and sunflowers (for making sunflower oil). Cattle, sheep, and pig farming have become increasingly important, while people in the northern tundra have herds of reindeer.

Fishing is important off the north coast and also in the Atlantic and Pacific oceans. Fishing vessels also operate in the Caspian Sea which contains sturgeon, which yield the delicacy caviar. But since the breakup of the Soviet Union in 1991, several nations now compete for this valuable product.

Above left: Fish experts examine sterlets, small sturgeon taken from the Amur River in eastern Siberia.

Below: A tea plantation in southern Kranoyarsk Region.

Above right: Harvesting grapes at Kuban in the southern part of the Krasnoyarsk Region of central Siberia.

Natural resources and industry

Before 1917, Russia was a backward country, whose economy depended mainly on agriculture. Under Communist rule, the Soviet Union became a leading industrial power. Russia has rich natural resources, including huge forests, abundant hydroelectric power, and many mineral deposits. Oil is extracted in several areas, including the Urals, the Sea of Azov, the Black Sea area, and western Siberia. The country has abundant iron ore and coal, which are used to make steel. Russia also has rich reserves of copper, gold, lead, platinum, tin, zinc, and various rare metals. Mines in Siberia produce large quantities of diamonds.

Much of Russia's manufacturing industry is based in the west, in European Russia. Moscow and St. Petersburg are leading manufacturing cities, while other industrial centers are situated along the Volga River and in the Ural Mountains region.

Above: Refining oil in Nizhnevartovsk. Russia has very rich natural resources and oil is extracted in many areas.

Left: Pouring molten steel at one of Russia's largest steel works at Magnitogorsk. This city is southwest of Chelyabinsk, in the southern Urals. It is a major industrial city.

Manufacturing is the most valuable activity in Russia. Under Communist rule, the government developed many state-owned industries, producing heavy machinery, tractors, and electrical equipment, as well as ships and other equipment. Chemicals, chemical products, and oil refining are also important. Processed food, paper, and textiles are other major manufacturing products.

After the breakup of the Soviet Union in 1991, Russia began to convert its government-controlled industries into privately owned ones. New businesses, some joint ventures with foreign companies, are being set up. Many new factories are making consumer goods, which were in short supply in the former Soviet Union. Russia has also obtained foreign technical assistance to modernize its older industries. This state of upheaval caused severe inflation, a fall in industrial production, and the collapse of some industries. Russia also faces another challenge — reducing the pollution caused by industry. Nevertheless, Russia's great natural resources and skilled workforce give hope for economic recovery.

Above: Open mining of coal at Kholboljinski mine in the Buryat Autonomous Republic, east of Lake Baikal. This region is rich in minerals, such as iron, titanium, and tungsten.

Below: Gold, mined in Yakutia, which has two of the country's major goldfields. Russia is one of the world's leading producers of this rare and valuable metal.

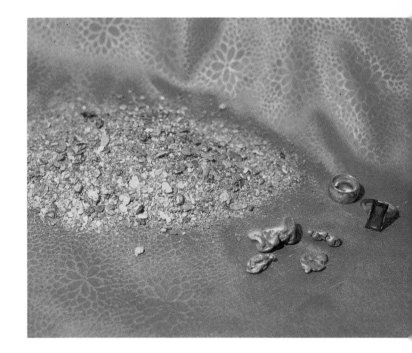

Soviet technology

In the years following World War II (1939–1945), Soviet technology concentrated on rebuilding its heavy industries, which had been destroyed or badly damaged by warfare. In the 1950s, Soviet technologists began to work on developing space industries. Several hundred spacecraft were launched every year. Most were artificial satellites intended for communications or meteorological purposes. There were also delivery supply flights carrying crews, food, water, and even fresh air to the country's orbiting space research stations.

The Soviet Union launched the first artificial Earth satellite, *Sputnik 1*, in October 1957. A month later, *Sputnik 2* carried a dog named Laika beyond the Earth's atmosphere. Two years later, *Luna 2* was the first space probe to land on the Moon. In 1961 Yury Gagarin (1934–1968), flying *Vostok 1*, became the first human to orbit the Earth.

Above: The Soviet ice-breaker Lenin was the world's first non-naval nuclear-powered ship.

Right: A Soyuz spacecraft blasts off to carry three Soviet cosmonauts into space. Some Soyuz missions have lasted for more than two months and made a thousand orbits of the Earth.

The Soviet Union scored several space "firsts." They included the first woman in space, Valentina Tereshkova (*Vostok 6*, 1963); the first docking of two crewed spacecraft and exchange of crews (*Soyuz 4* and *Soyuz 5*, 1969); and the launch of the first experimental space station (*Salyut 1*, 1971). In 1987–1988, Colonel Vladimir Titov and Flight Engineer Musa Manarov achieved the longest crewed space flight, lasting 365 days, 22.66 hours.

The breakup of the Soviet Union appeared to threaten the country's space research program because Baykonur, the Soviet space center from which all the crewed flights were launched, was in Kazakhstan, northeast of the Aral Sea. But in 1994, Russia agreed to rent the space center for twenty years.

Soviet scientists and technologists made many other important achievements. But in seeking to keep up in the arms race with the West, the Soviet Union diverted more and more of its efforts into military spending. This weakened the Soviet economy and was a major factor in the final collapse of the Soviet Union.

Above left: A giant MI-6 helicopter airlifts a portable building across difficult country for workers on the Baikal-Amur Mainline.

Above right: Colored lights trace out the movements of a cybernetic machine, or "robot."

Below: The Vilnisk power station is one of many hydroelectric projects being developed to meet the needs of Russian industry.

Transportation

The sheer size of Russia makes it essential to run an extensive and efficient system of transportation. For example, London is nearer to New York City across the Atlantic Ocean than Moscow in European Russia is to Vladivostok on the Pacific coast.

The Russian climate is unkind to roads. In the spring thaw, many road surfaces break up because of frost damage and become impassable seas of mud. Distances between major cities are long, and the country still has no major west-east highway link. Therefore, much freight is carried by rail instead of truck.

A rail line across Siberia, built between 1891 and 1916, links Moscow and Vladivostok. It runs close to the frontiers with Mongolia and China. In 1984, a new stretch of line was completed, running to the Amur River and the Pacific coast. This line is intended to open up the frozen, mineral-rich region north of Lake Baikal. It is known as the Baikal-Amur Mainline, or the BAM for short.

Private cars are expensive in Russia. But public transportation, including domestic flights, is inexpensive and good.

Above: Workers put the finishing touches to a new Vaz 2108 car.

Below left: Building the Baikal-Amur Mainline. The permafrost is so unstable that in places the railbed had to settle for two years before the trains could run over it.

Below: A modern high-speed express train waits at Volgograd station. More than half the rail network is electrified.

In parts of Russia, where the climate is less harsh, waterways are important in carrying goods and raw materials. The Volga, which flows into the Caspian Sea, is the main river used for transportation. Canals link it to the Baltic Sea, the River Don and the Sea of Azov, and also to the Moskva River and Moscow. Ice-breaking ships work to keep northern rivers and seaports open in winter, but most northerly ports become icebound and are closed between November and March.

The leading seaports include Archangelsk, Murmansk, Nakhodka, St. Petersburg, and Vladivostok. Another port, Kaliningrad, serves the small Russian enclave on the Baltic Sea between Poland and Lithuania. The Soviet airline Aeroflot was originally set up in 1923, and it became the largest airline of all time. But since 1990, the fleet has been operated by more than forty domestic operators.

Above: A station on the Circle Line of the Moscow Metro. This is the most elegant subway system in the world.

Below: A sleigh drawn by reindeer races over the snow near Murmansk, the country's chief Arctic Ocean port.

Fact file: economy and trade

▽ **The distribution of Russian economic activity**
Most industries and farming areas are in western
Russia. Siberia is comparatively underdeveloped.

	Industry
	Petroleum
	Natural gas
	Iron ore
	Coal

	Gold
	Cereals
	Potatoes
	Sugar beet
	Cotton

	Cattle
	Sheep
	Reindeer
	Forest products
	Fishing

Key Facts

Structure of production: Of the total gross domestic product, farming, forestry, and fishing contribute about 13 percent; industry 49 percent; and services 39 percent.

Farming: About 7 percent of the land in Russia is used for farming crops. Russia also has large areas of meadows and pastures for grazing. They make up about 5 percent of Russia. *Main products:* barley, eggs, fruits, dairy products, meat, milk, oats, potatoes and other vegetables, rye, sugar beet, sunflower seeds, wheat, wool.
Livestock: cattle, 54,700,000; sheep, 55,200,000; pigs, 35,400,000.

Forestry: Forests cover about 46 percent of the land. Not surprisingly, Russia is one of the world's leading producers of coniferous wood.

Mining: Russia's rich natural resources include oil, natural gas, and coal. It is also a major producer of copper, diamonds, gold, iron ore, platinum, lead, tin, zinc, and rare metals.

Transportation: *roads:* 554,900 miles (893,000 km), 74 percent paved; *vehicles* (1992): passenger cars, 9,661,000; trucks and buses, 465,000; *rail:* 98,241 miles (158,100 km); *airports* (1993): 58; *shipping:* the merchant marine carried 511 million tons (464 million tonnes) of cargo (1991).

Trade (1992): *Total imports:* U.S.$ 34,981 million; *exports:* U.S.$ 39,967 million.

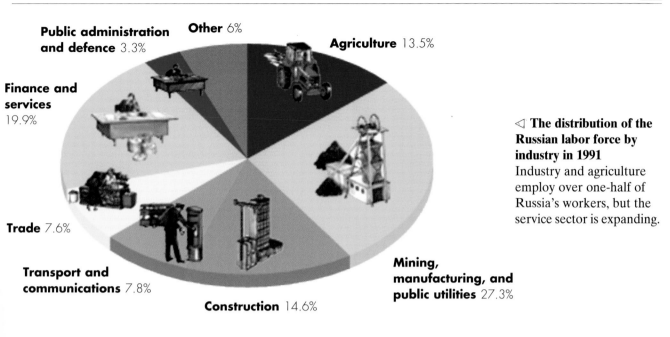

Public administration and defence 3.3%

Other 6%

Agriculture 13.5%

Finance and services 19.9%

Trade 7.6%

Transport and communications 7.8%

Construction 14.6%

Mining, manufacturing, and public utilities 27.3%

◁ **The distribution of the Russian labor force by industry in 1991** Industry and agriculture employ over one-half of Russia's workers, but the service sector is expanding.

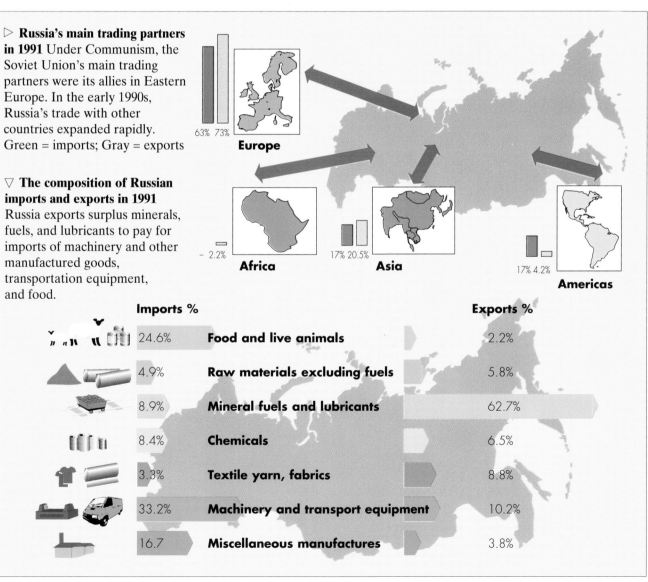

▷ **Russia's main trading partners in 1991** Under Communism, the Soviet Union's main trading partners were its allies in Eastern Europe. In the early 1990s, Russia's trade with other countries expanded rapidly. Green = imports; Gray = exports

63% 73% **Europe**

– 2.2% **Africa**

17% 20.5% **Asia**

17% 4.2% **Americas**

▽ **The composition of Russian imports and exports in 1991** Russia exports surplus minerals, fuels, and lubricants to pay for imports of machinery and other manufactured goods, transportation equipment, and food.

Imports %		Exports %
24.6%	Food and live animals	2.2%
4.9%	Raw materials excluding fuels	5.8%
8.9%	Mineral fuels and lubricants	62.7%
8.4%	Chemicals	6.5%
3.3%	Textile yarn, fabrics	8.8%
33.2%	Machinery and transport equipment	10.2%
16.7	Miscellaneous manufactures	3.8%

Education

Free, compulsory education is available for all children between the ages of seven and seventeen. Most children attend preschool kindergarten and continue further education after they are seventeen. Even remote areas have a full education service. Under Communist rule, all schools were run by the state. But in the 1990s, some private, fee-paying schools had opened. By 1992, Russia had about three hundred nonstate schools, with more than twenty thousand pupils, while some institutions of higher education had begun to charge tuition fees.

Most children attend school six days a week. The school day begins at 8:30AM and ends at 2:30PM. Pupils study basic subjects including Russian, though ethnic minorities have the right to teach in their own languages. Other basic subjects include mathematics, geography, history, social studies, and a foreign language (English is the most popular).

Above: A kindergarten playground in Moscow.

Below: Members of the Young Pioneers gather around a campfire at Bratsk, in Irkutsk.

Right: A Moscow secondary school student uses a computer during a mathematics lesson.

There are three types of secondary schools. Most pupils attend general secondary schools, where they add computer studies and more science subjects to their timetables. Particularly gifted pupils are selected for special secondary schools, where they receive extra tuition in such topics as art, music, languages or electronics. Vocational secondary schools concentrate on subjects, such as mathematics, chemistry, or physics.

Higher education is still somewhat elitist in Russia. Students in higher education are given a small allowance from the government. In the early 1990s, about 3,000,000 students were attending Russia's more than 500 higher educational establishments and more than 2,600 technical colleges.

Since the collapse of Communism, new curricula have been introduced. Textbooks and teachers now place less emphasis on political ideology. They have adopted a new approach to Russian and Soviet history, and previously banned literary works are now studied.

Above: Students attending a lecture at the M.V. Lomonosov State University in Moscow. The university was founded in 1755, and today has about 20,000 full-time students.

Below: The exterior of the M.V. Lomonosov State University in Moscow. It is generally regarded as the most prestigious of Russia's institutions of higher education.

The arts

Outside the country, the art of European Russia is best known, but the country has many cultures. In the northwest, the Sami (Lapps) carry on traditional handicrafts in bone and leather. In eastern Siberia, Mongol, Chinese, and even Japanese influences are apparent in painting, literature, and music.

The best-known Russian paintings are icons, religious pictures painted on wooden panels by artists of the Eastern Orthodox Church. In the early twentieth century, Russian artists developed modern styles. Under the Soviet government, artists were encouraged to use a straight-forward style, called "socialist realism," but today there is complete freedom for artists.

Russia is also known for its performing arts, especially ballet. State Kirov Academic Ballet of St. Petersburg and the Bolshoi Ballet of Moscow are world famous.

Above: A religious icon painting from the Solovetsky Cloister.

Left: A dancer with Moscow's Bolshoi Theater Ballet makes a spectacular leap. The world of ballet was dominated by Russia during the late 1800s and early 1900s.

Russian music is particularly noted for the operas of such composers as Modest Mussorgsky (1839–1881) and Nikolai Rimsky-Korsakov (1844–1908), and the ballet music of Peter Ilyich Tchaikovsky (1840-93) and Igor Stravinsky (1882–1971). Stravinsky, who like many other musicians left the Soviet Union, was one of the most influential twentieth-century composers. Sergei Prokofiev (1891–1953) and Dmitri Shostakovich (1906–1975) remained there.

The work of Anton Chekhov (1860–1904), the greatest Russian dramatist, has been translated into every major language. Fyodor Dostoyevsky (1821–1881) and Leo Tolstoy (1828–1910) were major novelists. Modern writers include Boris Pasternak (1890–1960) and Mikhail Sholokov (1905–1984). Alexander Solzhenitsyn (born 1918), who won the Nobel Prize for Literature in 1970, was exiled from Russia from 1974 to 1994.

Russian filmmakers include the director Sergei Eisenstein (1898–1948), whose *Potemkin* (1925) is a cinematic classic.

Above left: A member of the State Chorus of Kuban Cossacks.

Above right: A scene from *Ivan the Terrible* a film made in the 1940s by Sergei Eisenstein.

Below: Yevgeny Yevtushenko is a poet whose works commented on Soviet society.

The making of modern Russia

The Romanov family ruled Russia for more than 300 years. When the last Tsar, Nicholas II, was forced to abdicate in 1917, his country had hardly developed from a medieval, feudal state. The Tsars ruled as dictators. Most of the people were treated little better than slaves.

In 1914 Russia joined World War I against Germany and Austria. Nicholas took personal command of his armies, leaving the Tsarina Alexandra to rule. She was under the influence of a dissolute priest, Grigori Rasputin. Russia fell into chaos. Its armies lost battles, and food and fuel were scarce. Workers rioted and went on strike.

In March 1917 soldiers in the capital, Petrograd (now St Petersburg), mutinied. The Tsar was forced to abdicate, and a temporary government was set up. An exiled Communist, Vladimir Lenin (1870-1924), returned to Russia and seized power in a second revolution in November, helped by a group of Communists known as Bolsheviks. The Bolsheviks made peace with Germany in 1918. In 1922, they proclaimed the new Union of Soviet Socialist Republics (USSR), which included Russia.

Above: The last Tsar Nicholas II, who came to the throne in 1894, with the Tsarina Alexandra.

Below left: A crowd of Bolsheviks demonstrate.

Below: Vladimir Lenin led the Bolsheviks in the Russian Revolution of November 1917.

After the revolutions of 1917 the country was torn by civil war between the Red Army of the Bolsheviks, led by Lenin's second-in-command, Leon Trotsky, and the White Army of the anti-Communists. Lenin's Red Army won but Lenin died shortly after the new Soviet Union was proclaimed. The Communist secretary-general, Joseph Stalin (1879–1953), seized power.

Stalin introduced a brutal program of industrialization. Kulaks, wealthy peasant farmers, had their lands confiscated, and all farming was organized into collectives. Stalin's secret police removed all his political enemies. It is estimated that 20,000,000 people were murdered, tortured, or imprisoned without trial.

In 1941, during World War II, the Germans invaded the Soviet Union. Stalin and the Soviet armed forces played a major part in defeating Germany in 1945.

Above: Posters were often used to convey political messages. One (left) is a Bolshevik campaign poster; the other (right) remembers the starving.

Below: In 1945, just before the end of World War II, Stalin (right) met with Roosevelt of the United States and Churchill (left) of Britain to agree the post-war structure of eastern Europe.

Russia in the modern world

After 1945, the Soviet Union, suspicious of Western hostility toward Communism, determined that it would never again be invaded. An "arms race" developed between the Soviet Union, a world superpower, and its allies in Eastern Europe, and Western Europe, supported by the U.S., the other superpower.

A long period of hostility called the "cold war" began. But by the early 1980s, the high cost of financing the country's defenses crippled the Soviet economy. In 1985, Mikhail Gorbachev (born 1931) became the Soviet leader. He introduced new policies, including a new "openness" in government, called *glasnost*, economic reforms called *perestroika* (restructuring), and increased freedom of speech. The "cold war" came to an end and relations with the West improved.

Gorbachev's reforms led to debates about the future of the Soviet Union. Gorbachev wanted to keep the fifteen republics of the Soviet Union united. But in 1990, the governments of the republics declared that their laws took precedence over Soviet laws.

Above: The face of Russian cosmonaut Yury Gagarin, the first man to travel in space, dominates the Moscow Cosmos Space Pavilion.

Below: Mikhail Gorbachev, (far left), whose reforms led to debates about the future of the Soviet Union, receiving the Nobel Peace Prize in Oslo, 1990.

In August 1991, Communists tried to overthrow Gorbachev's government. But they were defeated by forces led by the Russian president, Boris Yeltsin (born 1931). Gorbachev remained Soviet president until December 25, 1991, when the Soviet Union was dissolved. Russia and the other 14 republics then became separate nations. Ties were maintained through a loose confederation called the Commonwealth of Independent States which, by 1994, contained all the former Soviet republics except for Estonia, Latvia, and Lithuania.

In Russia, Yeltsin, supported by Western governments, pushed ahead with reforms, though he had to put down another rebellion in October 1993. A new constitution was adopted in 1993 and multiparty, parliamentary elections were held. Though the reforms have caused upheaval, most experts believe that Russia, with its huge resources and skilled workforce, will overcome its current problems.

Above left: Crowds watch a tank near Parliament during the rebellion in October 1993.

Above right: A commercial bank. Experts believe that Russia's resources and skilled workforce will see it through its problems.

Below: American President Bill Clinton meets Boris Yeltsin in Moscow in January 1994.

Fact file: government and world role

The Commonwealth of Independent States is a loose confederation (union) of twelve of the fifteen republics which made up the former Soviet Union.

Key Facts

Official name: *Rossiyskaya Federatsiya* (Russian Federation) or *Rossiya* (Russia).

Flag: Tricolor: three horizontal stripes of white (top), blue (center), and red (bottom).

National anthem: No words; tune from an opera by Mikhail Glinka.

National government: Russia is a multiparty federal republic. The *head of state* is the directly elected president, who may not be elected to more than two four-year terms. *The president* is responsible for foreign policy and is commander in chief of the armed forces. The president may, under certain conditions, introduce martial law or a state of emergency. *The Federal Assembly* (parliament) contains two

houses. The upper house, the *Federation Council*, has 178 members, two from each of the republics, territories, provinces, autonomous areas, and cities of federal status, which together make up the Federation. The lower house, the *State Duma*, has 450 deputies elected to four-year terms. The *government* is made up of a chairman, nominated by the president and approved by the State Duma, a deputy chairman, and federal ministers.

Judiciary: Judges to the three highest courts are elected by the Federation Council, on presentation by the president. The Constitutional Court deals with constitutional matters, the Supreme Court with civil, criminal, administrative, and other matters, and the Supreme Arbitration Court, with economic and other disputes.

Local government: Local government is carried on by the 89 members of the Russian Federation through elected and other bodies.

Armed forces: A Russian army was created in 1992. By 1994, its strength was about 1,000,000, 450,000 of whom were conscripts. *Navy:* Russia inherited most of the Soviet fleet, but personnel and activities were greatly reduced in the early 1990s because of lack of funds; personnel in 1993 was 300,000, 180,000 of whom were conscripts. *Air Force:* Russia has an air force and air defense forces; personnel in 1993 totaled 400,000, 185,000 of whom were conscripts.

Alliances: Russia is a member of the United Nations, the UN Security Council, and the Council of Europe. In 1994, Russia signed the Partnership for Peace with NATO.

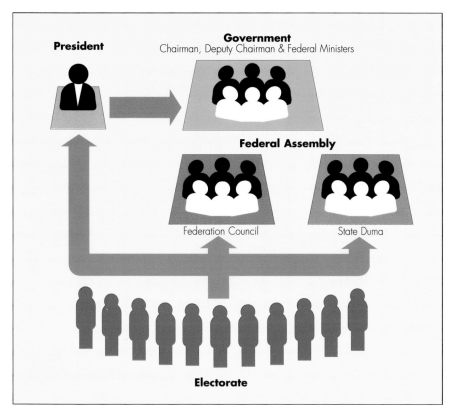

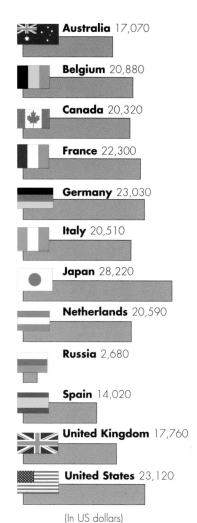

Australia 17,070

Belgium 20,880

Canada 20,320

France 22,300

Germany 23,030

Italy 20,510

Japan 28,220

Netherlands 20,590

Russia 2,680

Spain 14,020

United Kingdom 17,760

United States 23,120

(In US dollars)

△ **The Russian parliament**
Under Russia's constitution of 1993, the president, who is elected by direct suffrage for a term of four years, has sweeping powers.

▷ **National wealth created per person in 1992**
In 1992, Russia's economy was in a state of turmoil as state-run businesses were privatized and inefficient industries went out of business. This turmoil is reflected in Russia's low income per capita by comparison with Western countries.

△ **The Russian Federation**
Each of the eighty-nine regions of Russia sends two representatives to the Federation Council, the upper house in Russia's parliament.

Index